Acquitted

A Chronology of the Trump Years
Part Three

By John T Harding

By the same author:

Decline and Fall: A Chronology of the Trump Years
Law and the White House: Chronology Part Two
The Wolf Who Came Back
The Reluctant Shaman
The Puzzler
Jack and the Snark Angel
The Power of Twelve: And Other Scribblings
Druidry in America
Celtic Mythology
Druidry for Today: A Tradition Forgotten But Not Gone

Acquitted

A Chronology of the Trump
Years
Part Three

Independently published by John T Harding

Acquitted

By John T Harding

Prologue

The case against Donald Trump as president began long before he was elected and built steadily soon after he was inaugurated. Here's a rundown of some of the events and the background that led to this year's historic move.

Then after an 18-month gap, which is covered in Parts One and Two of this chronology, this volume resumes its documentation of Trump's impeachment.

Note: Even as the Senate trial began, he was pronouncing that if cleared of the charges, that will mean he was not impeached. Correction: It will only mean that he was not convicted. The word "impeached" will remain attached to his name forever.

This volume ends with a verdict of "not guilty" by the Senate and a defection from Republican ranks by Sen. Mitt Romney of Utah, who said his conscience would not allow him to clear the president of wrong-doing.

The following day, the president resumed his attack on critics with a rambling, vituperative victory speech, including an obscenity, to a packed crowd of supporters in the East Room of the White House. The speech was carried live on nationwide television.

Isolationism Redux
15 November 2015

No man is an island, entire of itself.
Neither is a nation.

Walls and blockades don't work. Trade does.

   The U.S. economy is approaching a healthy growth pace, but many other nations are stalled on the path to prosperity, including several important trading partners in Europe, Asia and Latin America.

   Even so, in the misguided belief that an isolated country is a secure country, conservatives are demanding protective walls, both physical and economic, to isolate America from the rest of the world.

   American isolationism failed in the 1920s and 1930s. In fact, the Smoot-Hawley tariff barriers only led to retaliation by other trading nations, and all sides suffered. Moreover, isolationist thinking at the time went hand in hand with bigotry and suppression of minority groups as well as efforts to replace democracy with authoritarianism. There have been at least three books published on that danger, only two of which were fiction: "It Can't Happen Here," by Sinclair Lewis (1935), "The Plot Against America," by Philip Roth (2004), and "The Plot to Seize the White House," by Jules Archer (1973). The first two are fictionalized novels of real possibilities, and the third documents a real conspiracy. All three deal with isolationist radicals of the 1930s who were determined to close all borders and build a Fortress

America.

Isolationist thinking fails to consider international reality.

The Great Wall of China, so highly praised by Donald J. Trump, was built by an emperor. The Iron Curtain and the Berlin Wall were built by Communist dictators. And the U.S. blockade of Cuba not only failed to overthrow the Castro regime, but also worsened the poverty of the Cuban people.

Erecting a wall to keep out Mexicans is not only impractical and racist (no Canadian wall has been suggested), but will only make things worse for America's southern neighbors.

If conservative politicians have their way and isolate the nation as a way to "retrieve" jobs from other countries and kickstart a surge in American manufacturing, the strategy may enjoy short-term success, but if the retrieved jobs are lost by other trading partners, those workers will be unable to buy. In short, an isolationist policy, like its mercantilist ancestor, is self-defeating. To think an isolationist economy can survive and thrive on its own is a pipe dream.

The Great Wall in China, the Iron Curtain and the Berlin Wall in Europe, as well as the Cuban Blockade, all throttled economic growth and severely harmed people's rights in all those insulated countries.

Walls and trade barriers are built by insecure dictators and repressive regimes unsure of their own security. They mislead their citizens into believing the folly that success comes in isolation.

That way madness lies.

It must not happen here
9 March 2016

Isolationism ignores reality.

"It can't happen here," you say? But it nearly did, at least twice before, and now a closed-border, isolationist America is once again being proposed.

The current political campaign is full of promises to "make America great again," shutting out those deemed undesirable, and shipping out those who somehow "don't belong."

The danger of such an attitude was raised in this space last November, months before the leading GOP candidate for the presidency began his current campaign.

"It Can't Happen Here," said Sinclair Lewis in his book of that title in 1935.

Philip Roth warned of "The Plot Against America" in his book published in 2004.

Both were fictionalized novels of real possibilities.

A third book, "The Plot to Seize the White House," written by Jules Archer and published in 1973, documented a real conspiracy by isolationist radicals of the 1930s who wanted to close all borders and build a Fortress America.

The Jules Archer book dealt with a plan by ultra-conservative corporate moguls to oust President Franklin D. Roosevelt and install their own leader.

A second attempt to subvert democratic channels and initiate full control by the White House was planned during the presidency of Richard M. Nixon, but it was foiled by close aides, led by senior advisor

Henry Kissinger.

All three of the books mentioned were based on events of the 1930s, when isolationist thinking and metaphorical wall-building in the form of high tariffs were riding high. At the time, the Smoot-Hawley tariff act imposed high fees on imports in a vain attempt to protect American products. But retaliation by other trading nations only raised prices for consumers everywhere, and all side suffered.

Recently, the leading contender for the Republican nomination insisted he would not only build a wall 40 feet high to keep out people from Mexico, but would impose a 35 percent tax on all products exported from that country to the U.S. as a way of paying for the wall.

But consider this: A wall stops travel from both sides, and a high tariff is added to the final sale price, imposing the cost of building on American consumers.

Moreover, as noted here last November, isolationist thinking at the time of the Great Depression "went hand in hand with bigotry and suppression of minority groups as well as efforts to replace democracy with authoritarianism."

Sound familiar?

Isolationist demagogues of the 1930s not only prolonged and worsened economic health of all sides, but also created conditions that led to war.

Unless voters reject another such xenophobic demagogue, it likely will happen here.

The Loser
10 October 2016

There are none so blind as those who will not see.

The storm warnings are there, and have been for many months, but it seems only now are Republican Party leaders acting on a pending disaster.

Increasingly, senior Republicans are saying they no longer can support their own nominee, claiming that his rantings about women, minorities, immigrants, the handicapped, religious groups and others do not represent what their party is about.

Really? The record shows otherwise. The difference is that Donald Trump has taken those positions to their natural extreme, and in the process has antagonized more people, more blatantly and in a shorter time than prior positions of other Republicans.

But perhaps the most dangerous political statement was the warning during Sunday's debate that as President he would appoint a special prosecutor to investigate his opponent's activities and see to it that she goes to jail. This reminded listeners of the "Lock her up!" chant heard at Trump campaign rallies.

That's the kind of political retaliation common to dictatorships around the world, but not found in America.

Yet.

Can it happen here? Is it possible, or even probable, that a demagogue can somehow take the low road to the White House and then wreak vengeance on his opponents?

Readers of this blog will remember that such a warning was posted four times since Trump became a national figure in presidential politics, most recently on 9 March of this year. Earlier comments were posted 20 October 2015, 21 September 2013, and 15 December 2012. Each posting cited two novels, one factual book and one true episode.

The novels are "It Can't Happen Here" (1935) by Sinclair Lewis, and "The Plot Against America" (2004) by Philip Roth. A third book, "The Plot to Seize the White House," written by Jules Archer and published in 1973, documented a real conspiracy by isolationist radicals of the 1930s who wanted to close all borders and build a Fortress America.

The Jules Archer book dealt with a plan by ultra-conservative corporate moguls to oust President Franklin D. Roosevelt and install their own leader.

A second attempt to subvert democratic channels and initiate full control by the White House was planned during the presidency of Richard M. Nixon, but it was foiled by close aides, led by senior advisor Henry Kissinger.

All three of the books mentioned were based on events of the 1930s, when isolationist thinking and metaphorical wall-building in the form of high tariffs were riding high. At the time, the Smoot-Hawley tariff act imposed high fees on imports in a vain attempt to protect American products. But retaliation by other trading nations only raised prices for consumers everywhere, and all sides suffered.

We now face an "America First" candidate who has borrowed that slogan from the isolationists of the 1930s and wants to build a real wall along the nation's southern border with Mexico and to expel millions of immigrants.

During Sunday evening's debate, Trump said that as President he would appoint a special prosecutor to pursue allegations of criminal behavior by the Democratic nominee, Hillary Clinton.

He made no mention, however, of the numerous formal legal charges pending against him about criminal behavior related to his business ventures. And despite much talk alleging criminal behavior by Mrs. Clinton, Congressional and FBI investigations have not found evidence enough to warrant formal charges.

Does this mean they don't exist? No, it only means they have not been found. On the other hand, plenty of evidence of Trump's questionable behavior -- both criminal and moral -- has been found.

But the final storm warning that caught the attention of GOP leaders was the release of recorded comments by Trump in which he bragged about his success in sexually assaulting women. "When you're a star, you can do anything," he boasted.

That was the last straw for many Republican leaders, who are now abandoning their own candidate, with some even calling for him to quit.

The term "quitter," however, does not seem to be in the Trump lexicon. Neither is "loser." But that, however, is what he is. Morally and ethically, he is already a loser. And come November, he is quite likely to be a political loser.

Meanwhile, an even bigger danger is that he and his supporters will not recognize the results of a nationwide general election, and will instigate some sort of rebellion. After all, he has already been warning that the election is being "rigged" against him.

What, then, will it take to convince him that he is, in fact, a loser?

It's Happening Here
24 May 2018

The death of Philip Roth reminded many of his novel, "The Plot Against America" (2004), which dealt with a conspiracy to overthrow the government. It was reminiscent of an earlier book by Sinclair Lewis, "It Can't Happen Here" (1935).

Meanwhile, a new book has hit the best seller lists dealing with the same theme. It's called "Fascism: A Warning," written by Madeleine Albright, former secretary of state and ambassador to the United Nations.

The difference is that the Albright book is true. It compares the characteristics of fascism as it rose in Europe in the 1930s to the actions, attitudes and strategies of the current occupant of the Oval Office today.

On Page 4 of her new book, Albright writes, "If we think of fascism as a wound from the past that had almost healed, putting Trump in the White House was like ripping off the bandage and picking at the scab."

Still another book," The Plot to Seize the White House," written by Jules Archer and published in 1973, documented a real conspiracy by isolationist radicals of the 1930s who wanted to close all borders and build a Fortress America.

Sound familiar? Build a wall. Keep out those somehow deemed undesirable, who don't speak the same language or follow the same religion as those already here.

Call them "animals," or somehow less than human, which enables a dominant group to exterminate them.

Sound familiar?

Neither Benito Mussolini nor Adolf Hitler were directly elected to power by a majority vote of the people. Both manipulated their national systems in order to gain control. Along the way, their speechifying and demagoguery planted the seeds of doubt on the land of truth.

That's another strategy used by would-be dictators on the fascist trail: Say something long enough, to enough people and loud enough to outshout those who speak and write information that exposes the lies, and eventually a demagogue will persuade enough people that he's right and everyone else is wrong. And with that leverage, the demagogue rises to power and strengthens his control.

And once in control, the new leader can eliminate by whatever means he can anyone opposed to his own version of "truth."

Sound familiar?

In America today, there are still enough people who recognize the tactics and strategies being deployed to erode and eliminate certain of the freedoms that people have long enjoyed, as guaranteed by the Constitution.

But already, there are undercurrents of movements to cancel the First Amendment by establishing a state religion, and to require that only adherents of a certain religion be admitted to America, thus wiping out Article VI of the Constitution itself.

Remember what it says? "No religious test shall ever be required as a qualification to any office or public trust under the United States."

Citizenship is a public trust. It is also a responsibility.

The Party's Over
17 July 2018

Watch for signs that the Republican Party in America is falling apart and may soon disappear.

Already, many GOP officeholders have decided to abandon any bid for re-election, and some incumbents are increasingly saying they oppose many of the actions of their party leader, President Donald Trump. In addition, government officials, including those appointed by Trump are resigning their positions rather than continue to serve their volatile leader.

The catch in the problem, however, is the strong loyalty shown by Trump's ever-loyal base of support.

As he proclaimed during the election campaign, "I could shoot someone in the middle of Fifth Avenue and not lose any voters."

This high confidence in the loyalty of his supporters, combined with a deep-seated sense of his own invincibility, combine to reinforce his conviction that he can do what he likes without consequences.

Complicating the issue is the possibility that he is somehow beholden to the Russian government and to Vladimir Putin, perhaps related to his financial dealings with government owned and controlled Russian banks. There have been solid reports that many Western banks stopped doing business with the Trump Organization after numerous defaults on construction loans. As a result, the company began taking out loans from other banks, allegedly benefitting from Moscow's need to find a way to launder money it acquired in other ways.

It has been suggested that this is one of the things that Putin is using to keep Trump in his pocket, forcing the American president to bend to the Russian leader's wishes.

In turn, this would explain why the normally boisterous Trump is overwhelmingly courteous in his comments about Putin, even as he boots his criticism of America's allies in Canada, Britain, France and Germany.

Details of Trump's financial dealings and allegations of money laundering won't fully be known until the president releases his tax returns, something he has steadfastly refused to do.

It remains possible, moreover, that investigators led by special counsel Robert Mueller will subpoena Trump's tax returns, thus harvesting the evidence to prove the president's involvement with foreign entities.

In turn, this could lead to criminal and/or impeachment proceedings, based on the constitutional ban on elected officials benefiting in any way from doing business with foreign companies or governments.

It's called the emoluments clause in the Constitution.

In addition, there is the Constitutional ban on "treason, bribery or other high crimes and misdemeanors," which is grounds for impeachment.

Already, numerous publications in America are using the T-word in their headlines about Trump's dealings with Putin.

Meanwhile, the Mueller probe obtained indictments of a dozen Russian intelligence officers charging them with working to invade the American voting system to help elect Trump.

The next question is, what American citizens did they work with in attempting to push the election to Trump's advantage?

Stay tuned.

While waiting, try reading "The Plot to Seize the White House," by Jules Archer; "The Plot Against America," by Philip Roth; and a new volume titled "The Plot to Destroy America," by Malcolm Vance.

Not to worry, some may say, because such a thing can't happen here.

Oh, right, that's another book title: "It Can't Happen Here," by Sinclair Lewis.

The reality is that it very nearly did, and if Americans are not vigilant, it may just happen.

Fortunately, the nation still has a vigilant and free press to continue warning of the danger, regardless of anyone's bombastic rantings about "fake news" perpetrated by journalists and news media that are labeled "the enemy of the people."

Yule Tidings
24 December 2019

Congress took a break for the holiday season, but that didn't stop them from sniping at each other on how to arrange the impeachment trial of the president.

So much for peace on earth to men (and women) of good will.

Nancy Pelosi, speaker of the House of Representatives, says she'll hold the articles of impeachment until there is some guarantee from the Senate that the trial will be fair and will hear from witnesses.

In reply, Senate leader Mitch McConnell says that's fine with him, don't send the documents at all, because Republicans don't want them anyway.

Meanwhile, President Donald Trump, target of the impeachment effort, says to bring it on right away, that he's ready to defend himself.

So now it looks like the Senate won't get a chance to consider the issue until mid-January, if then.

Holiday Brake
30 December 2019

The controversy over presidential impeachment slowed down as the year ended, but it will speed up as the election year leaps in.

Meanwhile, Republicans complained of how fast Democrats pushed the impeachment investigation and vote, leaving journalists to point out that the current process lasted about as long as the GOP took to impeach Bill Clinton -- a few months.

One difference is that Donald Trump was impeached during his first term as president, which prompted his supporters to claim that even if he is convicted by the Senate (highly unlikely as things are now, but that could change) and removed from office, he could still try for elective office again.

No, he couldn't. The Constitution is clear. But that doesn't stop Trumpians from chanting that claim many times.

It's an old strategy. Say something loud enough, long enough, to enough people often enough -- easy in this digital world of instant worldwide social media -- and some will start to believe it, partly because they get tired of hearing, so they start to think maybe it's true.

Doing it this way bypasses the mainstream media, whose job it is to expose misleading information and flat-out lies as soon as they appear.

The downside to this is that repeating a lie in the reporting on the strategy, even when exposing the lie, only gives it more exposure.

Besides, as Mark Twain once wrote, "A lie can travel halfway around the world while the truth is putting on its shoes." That's a variant on Jonathan Swift, who wrote in 1710, "Falsehood flies, and truth comes limping after it."

That's the predicament still faced by truth monitors in mainstream media today. Gossipers fly through the World Wide Web faster than journalistic fact checkers can turn on their computers.

Leaky Whistles
31 December 2019

As the year ended, the president joined several of his close companions in publicizing the name of the person they believe is the whistleblower who prompted the investigation that led to impeachment.

Never mind that his or her identity is protected by federal law and the alleged identity has never been supported by solid evidence from named sources, so the identity is not needed. Mainstream media, however, have followed the whistleblower protection law as well as their own policies and have not used the name.

But the president posted the name on his Twitter account, so millions of readers around the world know it. Add to that the not-so-subtle threats and implied suggestions by the Trump clan, and the result is the whistleblower's safety is at risk -- perhaps even endangering his/her life.

That doesn't seem to bother the Trumpistas. In fact, it may even be their plan. As long as someone else does the deed, they can insist on their right of free speech. As Pug Mahoney would say, however, "Your civil rights end where my toes begin."

In any case, retaliation like that is no longer civil. It's criminal.

So now comes in another legal issue: Incitement to violence. If something happens to the alleged whistleblower -- despite there being no solid evidence that he/she is who the Trumpistas say -- those who spread the name could be subject to criminal charges.

This would be even more criminal if the name broadcast is not, in fact, the name of the person who touched off the impeachment investigation.

Oops. Never mind.

That won't work, gang. You guys indirectly cause severe harm -- social at least and physical at worst -- to another human being.

Hiding behind "executive privilege" after causing violence or death won't be enough.

"Preemptive Self Defense"
4 January 2020

Someone counted the number of times Donald Trump accused President Barack Obama of planning to start a war with Iran in order to get re-elected.

Now we see Trump launching "pre-emptive self defense" against Iran just as re-election season begins. It's not an attack, he insists, and is meant to prevent war, not start one.

So how come it's OK for him but not the other guy?

Surely it's only a coincidence that this will distract from the impeachment hassle and call for patriotic Americans to put that issue aside, support the war effort and re-elect the current president.

Sure it is.

2020 Foresight
4 January 2020

Few people have 20/20 hindsight, and even fewer have 2020 foresight. Nevertheless, many try to predict what the future holds, using what logicians call the "ceteris paribus" assumption. That's Latin for "other things equal," and assumes that nothing changes.

A heroic assumption, at best, because things always change, and you never know which element will change, when, where, why, what will cause it, how and by how much.

There we are with those pesky Five Ws again.

Even so, the "ceteris paribus" assumption is useful, because you never know which element will change or when or by how much. Several months may go by and nothing happens, or there can be a rush of change by one or several elements of reality, leading to victory by the forces of chaos.

Agent 86 would not be surprised.

Anyway, given the events of recent weeks, and assuming governments continue the attitudes and strategies they have shown, it would be a fair assumption that chaos will reign in the Middle East and could well spread to the U.S., though probably not to the level of outright war.

Check the number of "if" phrases in the preceding paragraph. I count four.

So it's up to journalists to try to keep track of what's happening now, what caused the happenings, and what the consequences will be, as well as reporting what politicians and government officials have to say about what they plan to do about it, how, when and why.

Again with the Five Ws.

But it's part of the job, and will remain so as long as government doesn't succeed in controlling what the news media report. Not that they won't keep trying.

They have in the past and will in the future.
  Danger, Will Robinson!

Judgment Daze
10 January 2020

  Still waiting for documents to go to the Senate for
trial of the impeached president.
  Senate Leader Mitch McConnell, a Republican and
a supporter of the president, says he may go ahead
and start the trial anyway, even without the
impeachment documents drawn up by the House of
Representatives. And he suggests that he and the
GOP majority in the Senate will conduct the trial
without bothering to call any witnesses.
  So if there are no formal charges, no witnesses or
testimony, and comments only from the defense and
supporters of the impeached president, that yields no
meaning to the supposed "trial," and it becomes a
sham, to use one of the president's favorite words.

Status Quo Quiz
11 January 2020

  The Senate is likely to get impeachment documents
this week, but that's not fully clear. House Speaker
Nancy Pelosi said she would name trial managers to
present the case to the Senate, but that's doesn't
mean they will immediately forward the articles of
impeachment. More likely, they will say they need
time to review the documents, as well as more recent
information that has come out, and to plan strategy
on how best to present the case, especially since

Senate leaders say they don't want it anyway.

Never mind what the Constitution says.

GOP senators are working closely with the White House on a defense strategy, so the idea of congressional independence is moot for now.

Will it return? If so, when? Perhaps when senators remember their constitutional obligation to uphold the checks and balances required in a democratic society and government.

By the way, have you noticed that members of the Republican Party refer to their opposition as members of the "democrat party"? This implies that the party is not really "democratic."

Copy editors will note that the name of the party is capitalized -- Democratic Party -- and the name of the tradition -- democratic -- is not.

Perhaps some will retaliate by using the term "repo party."

Timeline
14 January 2020

Republicans have complained early and often about the timeline involved in completing the impeachment process. So let's compare the timelines set by the GOP when President Bill Clinton was impeached.

From the day Clinton denied having sex with "that woman" (Jan. 26, 1998) to the day the House of Representatives impeached him for "lying to Congress" about the affair (Dec, 19, 1998), nearly a full year went by.

The case was forwarded to the Senate, where a

trial began Jan. 7,1999. The president was acquitted on Feb. 12, 1999.

The investigation of Donald Trump was shorter, but considering the egregious nature of the allegations, it's not hard to understand the speed of collection.

Moreover, there was less resistance from the White House during the Clinton probe. This is not to say there was great cooperation, but the Administration did not order all staffers to refuse to testify about anything at any time, under any circumstance.

That reflects the Trump attitude about his affairs, ranging from his college grades to his income and his business relationships while in office. He refuses all, even the information that would document just how his personal business interests benefit from his presidential activities.

He keeps insisting that everything is fine and totally legal, but given his documented history of prevarication on so many things so often, there is little to no reason we should believe him now.

The sad thing is that so many of his supporters say we should believe the president because he is the president, and for no other reason.

A classic example of circular logic.

Any suggestion that they should have supported Barack Obama for the same reason is dismissed because "that's different."

How and why it's different is never explained.

The House Intelligence Committee began impeachment hearings on Nov. 13, 2019, after many months of public talk about the need to remove Donald Trump as president.

After several weeks of hearing testimony, the House Judiciary Committee approved two articles of impeachment on Dec. 12. The following week, on Dec. 18, the House of Representatives formally impeached the president.

The next move will be for House Speaker Nancy Pelosi to name managers for the impeachment trial. That's expected this week, and the Senate trial could begin as early as the next day.

Is the process rushed, as Republicans claim? Talk of impeaching Trump began even before he was inaugurated, and there were several motions quickly made in Congress to begin the process, but Speaker Pelosi sidelined most of them, until the Intelligence Committee began its hearings last November, three years after Trump was elected.

Sufficient evidence to justify impeachment was readily available, and continues to pile up even as the trial is about to begin. Now the question is whether the Republican-dominated Senate will accept any evidence or will it move to dismiss the charges on Day One.

Busy News Day
15 January 2020

It was a busy news day today.

House Speaker Nancy Pelosi named seven prosecution managers to handle the Trump impeachment, and the full House voted along party lines to send to the Senate, which was done later in the day.

The prosecution team will be led by Adam Schiff of

California, chairman of the Intelligence Committee, and Jerrold Nadler of New York, chairman of the Judiciary Committee.

Separately, more evidence has come out documenting the president's pressure on Ukraine -- through his lawyer Rudy Giuliani -- to intervene in the American election. Meanwhile, Republicans in the Senate are increasingly dissatisfied with the president's strategy on the Iran issue, and the chamber is likely to put limits on his war powers. Whether the president will veto such an act is something to watch for.

House members are still challenging the Senate to call witnesses in the trial. Nadler said, "Any trial that does not allow witnesses is not a trial, it is a coverup."

There has also been talk that the Senate will dismiss the allegations even before hearing evidence, prompting House Speaker Nancy Pelosi to say, "Dismissal is a coverup."

The entire process is in large part a reaction to the president's attitude displayed in his comment that "Article II of the Constitution says I can do whatever I want."

A careful read of that part of the Constitution indicates no such thing. Try it.

The document starts by specifying that "The executive Power shall be vested in a President ... (who) shall hold his office during the term of four years," and it specifies how the president be elected.

Next is a list of qualifications for a candidate. That the candidate be a "natural born citizen" (not native born; if one parent is a citizen, the child is a citizen no matter where born), and the candidate be 35 years of age and a resident of the United States for 14 years.

Section 2 then specifies the powers a president has, mostly dealing with appointments and nominations.

Section 3 directs that the president "give to the Congress information on the State of the Union, and recommend to their consideration such measures as he shall judge necessary and expedient."

Note the phrase "recommend to their consideration." This is not to say the Congress must obey.

Finally, Section 4 stipulates that "the president, vice president and all civil officers of the United States shall be removed from office on impeachment for, and conviction of, treason, bribery or other high crimes and misdemeanors."

That last paragraph is what brings the news of the day to the fore. Nowhere in the section dealing with the presidency does the Constitution say, hint or suggest that person holding the office has unlimited powers.

That would be a dictatorship or a monarchy, which is what caused America to declare its independence in 1776.

And at root, that is what precipitates the current crisis -- to prevent a dictatorship in America.

Solemnity Takes Charge
16 January 2020

The Senate chamber was quiet today as the impeachment trial of Donald Trump got under way.

There was very little chatting and 99 of the 100 seats were filled as senators heard the articles of impeachment being read, then listened as John Roberts, chief justice of the United States Supreme Court, arrived to be sworn in and preside over the impeachment trial.

Then each senator answered individually to live up to the oath, and then lined up to sign the oath book. One senator was absent for family illness reasons and will be sworn in later.

The formality was solemn. Only twice before in the nation's history has the senate held a trial to determine whether a president should be convicted of the charges against him, removed from office and prohibited from holding other office of public trust in America.

As the formalities ended, Chief Justice Roberts adjourned the proceedings until next week.

Meanwhile, the evidence supporting the case against the president continued to pile up, as more documentation became public that he broke the law by withholding military aid to Ukraine in exchange for support in his re-election campaign. Leading this was a report from the Government Accountability Office specifying that he violated federal law in doing so. The GAO has a solid reputation for being nonpartisan and accurate. Nonetheless, the White House rejected the GAO conclusion.

Now it will be up to the Senate to decide whether to accept the GAO report as evidence, and to decide whether to believe the GAO or accept the president's denial.

The Party Nears Its End
17 January 2020

Life is a series of if-then statements.

The fun and games of political sniping ended as the Senate began the impeachment trial of the current president of the United States, Donald Trump.

The larger question, however, is whether this will see the end of his presidency if he is convicted and removed from office, or whether -- if he is cleared by the GOP dominated Senate -- this will mean the end of the Republican Party.

As early as October 2016, a month before the presidential election, this blog noted the storm warnings that the party was heading for disaster, and spoke of "the kind of political retaliation common to dictatorships around the world, but not found in America."

The question posed then was whether "a demagogue can somehow take the low road to the White House and then wreak vengeance on his opponents."

Monday will mark exactly three years since Trump was inaugurated, and Tuesday will see the active beginning of his impeachment trial in the Senate.

This is an historic time, and the next few weeks will reveal whether the system works, or whether a demagogue can succeed in dominating the government for his own benefit.

If Trump is convicted and removed from office -- assuming he actually does leave or must be physically forced out -- we will know the system works. But if the Senate fails to convict, despite all the evidence pointing to guilt, we may well face turmoil never before seen in America. And that is likely to mean the end of the Republican Party.

It can't happen here, you say?

But it very nearly did, several times, as written about in the actual attempt to oust President Franklin D. Roosevelt, documented by Jules Archer in his book, "The Plot to Seize the White House," published in 1973. And there is the novel "It Can't Happen Here," by Sinclair Lewis, a fictionalized version of the same attempt, as well as "The Plot Against America," by Philip Roth. More recently, there is Madeline Albright's book warning of the danger of "Fascism" encroaching in America.

All this can be avoided if the Senate, currently dominated by Republicans who support the president, decides to convict him of the charges leveled against him and orders him removed from office.

If they do not, then we may see the end of the Republican Party.

Life is a series of if-then statements.

Electoral College Dropout
17 January 2020

Watch for the electoral college to be flunked out of the presidential process.

The Supreme Court has agreed to hear two cases challenging the way delegates vote for presidential candidates, and may require all states to side with one method.

Most states require electors to vote for the candidate with the most popular votes, but there are others that leave the choice to individual electors. As it is, the presidential candidate with the higher popular vote can still lose the Oval Office seat as the electoral college vote goes to the competition.

That has already happened several times, including Donald Trump's victory in the electoral voting despite having lost the nationwide popular vote to Hillary Clinton.

The Constitution only says that voters in the several states choose electors, who then meet to select a president. It does not require that electors follow the popular voting choice. That may be a reflection of the times, when those who wrote the Constitution did not fully trust the general population.

Some states do require its electors to follow the popular choice, which makes the procedure little more than a formality. Other states, however, allow delegates to the electoral college to vote as they please, regardless of the will of the majority population.

Challenges in two states have resulted in differing judgements in federal appeals courts, so it now falls to the Supreme Court to decide which method best follows the intent of the founders.

It's not clear yet just when the Supreme Court will hear arguments in the case, nor whether the issue will be decided in time for next November's presidential voting.

Moot Bluster
20 January 2020

"Dangerous attack ... brazen and unlawful ... highly partisan and reckless obsession."

That's in just the first paragraph of the president's response to articles of impeachment sent to him by the Senate. It goes on like that for another five pages, but without any specific details.

Maybe that will come from witnesses when the trial gets under way. Then again, maybe not, since Trump and his defenders have refused every request and blocked every attempt to force witnesses to testify in his defense as the investigation went through the House.

And whether the Senate will call witnesses is an open question. The Republican leadership has insisted that the charges have no merit and the case should be immediately dismissed. But if the GOP calls any defense witnesses, that will mean the Democratic accusers will also be able to call witnesses.

There is also the reality that if defenders do call witnesses, they will be under oath and would face punishment if they are not truthful. Meanwhile, defenders can say whatever they like in news media and other public forums, since they will not be under oath and there is no outright legalistic punishment for lying to the press and the public.

Pound the Table
22 January 2020

The impeachment trial got off to another blustery

start today, with Democrats laying out the chain of evidence calmly but Republicans responding by attacking the process.

It reminded me of the lawyer's maxim: When you have the facts on your side, argue the facts. When you have the law on your side, argue the law. When you have neither, pound the table.

There has been a lot of table pounding as the GOP blocked every proposed amendment Democrats put forth on how to conduct the trial and how and when to introduce evidence and hear witnesses.

Republicans are looking to dismiss the case without hearing evidence or witnesses. If they succeed, it will mean serious trouble for a democracy and a big opportunity for an autocrat.

Unless, of course, he loses re-election. He rigged the last one by way of the electoral college, and unless the Supreme Court ends that way of choosing a president, he will try again later this year.

Tumbling Down
24 January 2020

Note to Senator Ostrich: When your head is buried in the sand, you can't complain about the dark.

The Administration's stone wall may be crumbling from the barrage of evidence presented to the Senate in the president's impeachment trial.

Republicans do their best to block every attempt to bring witnesses to the trial and to present new evidence that has been found since the president was impeached, but this only repeats the question:

If you're innocent, you have nothing to hide, and if you have nothing to hide, why are you concealing evidence? Especially if, as you claim, it would prove your innocence?

Likely answer: The evidence would further prove guilt, and that's why you're stonewalling investigators.

But the stone wall is crumbling as prosecutors show many video clips from House hearings as well as TV appearances, which show in detail the president's actions and comments about incidents that brought on the investigation and impeachment.

House impeachment managers shed light every day on the actions and comments of the president and his aides as well as government staffers in support of the charges.

So far, however, the defense strategy has been to attack the process rather than give evidence to repudiate the charges.

Could it be that any evidence they do give would actually support the charges, and that's why the White House refuses to cooperate with investigators, even to the extreme of defying Congressional subpoenas?

Presumed innocent until proven guilty, of course, but the evidence of guilt keeps piling up. Defense lawyers claim "executive privilege," so the subpoenas were not valid. Moreover, some of the subpoenas were withdrawn, which they claim proved they were not valid.

They neglect to mention that a court challenge of the congressional subpoenas would drag out the process for months, so investigators decided to go ahead with the evidence they already had.

In a way, they yielded to the GOP demand to move quickly in the impeachment process. But you can't always have things both ways. Either you help speed up the process or you keep challenging every step, thus prolonging the process.

Ignorance is Bliss
24 January 2020

Interesting to note that the Fox cable news network is not carrying the Senate impeachment hearings, instead showing its squadron of pro-Trump commentators. Could it be that the evidence is too strong for them, and they have chosen to ignore it?

Pompeo Pomposity
25 January 2020

Never pick a fight with someone who buys ink by the barrel. Or who has a broadcast license. And especially someone who is a news anchor for NPR and has degrees from Harvard and the University of Cambridge and who worked for the BBC before returning to America.

All these cautionary mottos were ignored by Secretary of State Mike Pompeo as he stormed out of an interview with Mary Louise Kelly, host of NPR's program "All Things Considered." And because he did not like the questions, he salted his abuse of Kelly with obscenities, according to numerous reports. After he left, aides wanted to take her recording of the interview.

NPR has a solid, well deserved reputation for

neutral, objective reporting of the news, and the program Kelly hosts is a prime example of that reputation.

Clearly, Pompeo did not like the questions Kelly was asking. Tough tacos, mate. Journalists ask questions that need to be asked, and while there may be some news outlets that have a bias in favor of a certain political standpoint (you know who they are), NPR is not one of them.

The operation is publicly supported, and runs no commercial advertising. It reports news clearly and concisely, without regard to any political viewpoint. And much as the current White House inmates want favorable (read: propaganda) coverage from every news outlet, the very last one to fall into that trap would be NPR.

So be careful whom you insult, politicos, because that only means sharper pencils. And more air time to expose abusive behavior.

Defensive Opening
27 January 2020

Pressure on the Senate is building to hear witnesses as more evidence is presidential behavior and actions becomes public.

This, even as his defense team begins its presentation to the Senate, primarily attacking the process but insisting that even if he did do what he is accused of doing, there is nothing wrong or illegal about it and is therefore not impeachable.

Note: He was in fact impeached. As of today, he has not been convicted.

Meanwhile, published reports document just how, when and with whom the president met to plan withholding of aid to Ukraine unless its government announce an investigation of political opponents.

Note that the demand does not call for an actual investigation; just an announcement of one.

Former presidential aide John Bolton has written a book about his White House days, and the New York Times obtained a copy in advance of its publication date some two months from now.

By that time, however, the impeachment trial likely could be over, so the book would have no influence on the verdict. But the breaking news has brought more calls for direct testimony from Bolton, and has led some Republicans to waver in their solidarity with party leadership.

Bolton has said he is willing to talk to Congress if subpoenaed. In the past, however, the White House has not only defied subpoenas and told staffers not to respond, but has also gone to court to delay them.

However, rather than spend many more weeks -- if not months -- fighting court battles over subpoenas, House investigators decided to proceed with whatever solid information they had, and they withdrew the subpoenas.

But now defenders seize on that withdrawal as proof of weakness in the case. In doing so, they ignore all the other evidence presented to the Senate.

Defenders have said repeatedly that it was the duty of the House to do all the investigating and gather all the evidence. At the same time, they stressed the importance of a swift probe and a rapid trial, even as they used many delaying tactics.

In doing all that, they ignore the historical reality that the Senate did its own investigating in prior impeachment cases. This tactic is also an attempt to ignore new evidence that was previously suppressed by the White House.

And that in itself -- obstruction of a Congressional investigation into presidential actions and behavior -- is an impeachable offense.

Quick Wrap Up
28 January 2020

The impeachment defense wrapped up its presentation to the Senate today, without really contesting any of the evidence presented but focusing more on the process, claiming it did not meet the standard of an impeachable offense.

And as they have in previous presentations, they used the term "impeached" in a way that suggests the president cannot be considered impeached until and unless he is convicted of the charges against him.

That's curious, because they do not plan on calling any witnesses to rebut the testimony. Strategically, that means that if they do call a witness, then those who brought the charges will have the same right to call witnesses.

Meanwhile, the flap over the new book by John Bolton continues to dominate the news cycle, and the Senate now faces a decision on whether to accept Bolton's comments as part of the trial proceedings.

He has expressed a willingness to testify if he is

subpoenaed. But if the Senate does issue a subpoena, the White House is likely to challenge it in court, which would drag out the process well into the election season.

There is also the question of whether the presiding chief justice can or will overrule the subpoena. In turn, that could be overturned by a majority vote of the Republican-dominated Senate.

So the bottom line question remains this: If he is innocent, as he claims, why hide the evidence that would prove it? Instead, it appears that the defense team blocks every move to obtain any documentation from the White House, claiming "executive privilege."

That, however, brings up a legal point: Does executive privilege apply to hiding criminal behavior?

One Sided Peace Treaty
28 January 2020

President Trump and Israeli Prime Minister Benjamin Netanyahu announced a peace plan for the West Bank, but the Palestinian leadership was not part of the announcement.

This announcement came just hours after Netanyahu was indicted on three charges of corruption -- bribery, fraud and breach of trust -- in an Israeli court.

The treaty guarantees Israel control of a unified Jerusalem and does not call for Israeli settlements in the disputed area to be abandoned.

Trump called the plan "a win-win for both sides," but whether it means Israel now has American support to annex the area is sure to be debated.

Israel has occupied the territory since the 1967 war, when it took the region away from Jordan. Since then, Palestinians have fought for their independence or at least equal treatment from the Israeli government.

Word Warriors
29 January 2020

"I'm not a lawyer, but I know what words mean." -- Pug Mahoney
"My words mean just what I choose them to mean, neither more nor less." -- Humpty Dumpty
"How can you make words mean so many different things?" -- Alice
"The question is, which is to be master, that's all." -- Humpty Dumpty
"Therefore, you won't know what his words mean until he tells you what they mean." -- Pug Mahoney

Lawyers argue the meanings of words and, like Humpty Dumpty, claim they alone are the masters and others -- non-lawyers -- cannot know the meanings until and unless a lawyer explains them.

But others do know the meanings of words. They are teachers, writers, journalists, linguists, lexicographers and everyone else who is fluent in a given language. Especially educated native speakers.

For example, you don't need a college diploma to know that lying is wrong.

We see a classic example these days of legalistic maneuvering and debate as defenders of the current president argue to the Senate that even if he did do some or all of the things he is accused of in the articles of impeachment, such things are done all the time, and therefore they do not meet the standard of a high crime or some other misdemeanor.

In an odd way, the lawyers are not denying that the president may in fact have perpetrated some of the things he is accused of doing, but if he did, they are covered by "executive privilege" and therefore are not crimes, and even if they are, he does not have to talk about them and that's why he's withholding documentary evidence and forbidding his aides to testify about them.

Moreover, that's not obstruction, that's executive privilege.

Around and around it goes. Can you say "circular logic"? I knew you could.

It goes like this: It's true because I say it's true, so that resolves the debate and ends the discussion. Therefore we don't need evidence or testimony because my word is enough.

In New Jersey, that's called BS -- Blowing Smoke.

Say What?
29 January 2020

"When the president does it, it's not illegal." -- Richard Nixon

"I could shoot somebody in the middle of Fifth Avenue and not lose any votes." -- Donald Trump

"Article Two of the Constitution says I can do

whatever I want." -- Donald Trump.

   "If the president does something he believes will help him get elected," that's in the public interest and is not impeachable, according to defense attorney Alan Dershowitz in answer to a senate question.
   Dershowitz, a Harvard law professor, also maintained that the events documented in the articles of impeachment do not allege a crime, and therefore are not impeachable, much less grounds for removal from office.
   And even if the events were criminal, other defense lawyers insist, such things are done all the time and therefore are not impeachable.
   Soon it will be up to senators to decide whether the allegations are, in fact, criminal and if not whether they are an abuse of power and therefore warrant conviction and removal from office.

Suspense Ending
30 January 2020

   The Senate impeachment trial may be nearing an end, with increasing speculation on whether witnesses will be called to endorse or defend the charges against the president.
   If not, Democrats will charge "coverup," and the trial will end with a likely acquittal.
   If so, Republicans will also call witnesses, including former Vice President Joe Biden and his son Hunter, in an effort to distract senators from the core issues in the trial -- whether President Trump broke the law in threatening to withhold aid to Ukraine unless its

president announces an investigation of the Bidens.

If witnesses are called, the trial would drag on for days or weeks, and if the Trump team takes the issue to court, delay could well be months.

The General Accounting Office (GAO) reported that it was a violation of law to withhold aid that that Congress had already approved, thus supporting the charge of extortion. The Republican defense has been that the aid was later released, so it did not matter. Legal experts, however, point out that even a threat of extortion is illegal, even if the threat is later withdrawn.

Meanwhile, the White House is setting up rallies across the country to demonstrate popular support for the president and for his GOP allies who are up for election.

An example would be a rally this week in Wildwood, NJ, where hopeful attendees camped out on the beach boardwalk overnight to be sure of getting a seat. Reminder: It's mid-January.

Congressional Copout
31 January 2020

Yes, he did it, but we don't care. Let the voters decide.

That seems to be the crux of the Senate Republican attitude toward the impeachment issue as a party line vote dismissed a bid to call witnesses and see documents that would support -- or defend against -- the allegations against the president. The vote was 51-49.

"This is the greatest coverup since Watergate," said Sen. Chuck Schumer (D-NY), calling the episode "a sham." Moreover, when there are no witnesses and no documents, that means there is no trial, he added.

Rep. Adam Schiff (D-CA), an impeachment manager, said, "A trial without witnesses is no trial at all."

The opposite view was summarized by Sen. Lamar Alexander (R-Tenn), who said the Senate should acquit the president of the charges against him and leave the decision to voters.

"The question then is not whether the president did it, but whether the United States Senate or the American people should decide what to do about what he did," Alexander said in a written statement. "Let the people decide," he added.

So the next critical vote is likely to be next Wednesday, when the Senate will consider whether to dismiss the charges and acquit the president. Coincidentally, that day happens to be the same day he is scheduled to deliver the State of the Union message.

One can only guess whether that will actually happen, and if it does, whether he will claim absolute and total vindication during the speech.

But the evidence remains, and continues to pile up. Eventually, the whole truth will come out.

Acquittal Equals Approval
2 February 2020

Acquittal equals approval.
That's the conclusion of the Trumpistas, so not only

will the president continue what he has been doing, but is likely to accelerate what he says and does in governing the country.

Moreover, it will mean that he alone governs the nation, and Congress has sublimated itself to a secondary role and is bound to do what he says.

Strict Constitutionalists will disagree, of course, and that will be a core issue in the upcoming presidential election, which is only nine months away.

Unlike other court proceedings, where a "not guilty" verdict means the accusations were not proven beyond a reasonable doubt, and does not translate to "innocent," Republican supporters of the president admit that he did in fact say and do the things listed in the articles of impeachment, but they insist it doesn't matter.

He is the president, they say, and is allowed a broader range of behavior than other citizens.

Or, the president himself has said, "I can do whatever I want."

This contrasts with the Democrats' argument, voiced many times in recent weeks, that no one is above the law. And major media outlets have increasingly compared his attitude to that of King Louis XIV of France: "I am the state." Or, as used by The New Yorker magazine: "L'etat, c'est Trump."

This week will fill news pages easily. The president recorded an interview with Fox commentator and Trump supporter Sean Hannity, being broadcast the same day as the professional football Super Bowl game.

Monday will see closing arguments about impeachment in the Senate, as Iowans caucus to express the presidential preferences, Tuesday the president is scheduled to deliver his state of the union address, and on Wednesday, the Senate is scheduled for a final vote on impeachment.

Wonder what the president will say about his trial?

By the way, what does it say about a man who always mocks his opponents about their height? The latest is Democratic candidate Mike Bloomberg. What's more important, a person's intelligence and abilities or the size of his ... whatever?

Gloat Rack
3 February 2020

Look for the Senate to formally censure the president for what members have called "inappropriate behavior" as described in the articles of impeachment.

Senators will likely do this rather than find him guilty of the charges, which would remove him from office and forbid him from holding any other federal office in the future.

Republicans have said he probably did do the things he was accused of doing, but they claimed the actions and comments did not rise to the level of "high crimes and misdemeanors" that impeachment calls for.

Therefore, Republican thinking goes, convicting him of the charges would be too extreme. Not only that, but observers suggest that doing so would be a concession to Democrats that they were right, and politically that would be too much for them to deal with in this election year.

This will depend partly on what, if anything, the president says about the impeachment trial during his State of the Union address to the nation Tuesday evening. A Senate vote on whether to convict him of the impeachment charges is scheduled for Wednesday.

So if he gloats of his victory the day before it happens, that may be the final straw for reluctant Republicans to bear. And rather than convict him and oust him from office -- a first for the nation -- Senators would censure him as a way to avoid the issue and "let the voters decide" on Election Day in November whether he stays in office.

Four More Years?
5 February 2020

Supporters chanted "Four more years" as the president began his State of the Union address to a joint session of Congress Tuesday evening.

It was just one of the signals Team Trump sent to the conservative base that their leader wants to stay on the job.

But perhaps the strongest signal was when Trump awarded the presidential Medal of Freedom to Rush Limbaugh, the ultra-conservative talk show host with an audience of millions. The award was made live on national television during the speech.

The award came one day after Limbaugh announced that he has stage four cancer.

Awarding the nation's highest civilian honor to Limbaugh live during prime time on national television will certainly please conservatives, but liberals will see it as a political ploy to distract from the impeachment issue and refocus voter attention on re-election.

Next comes a vote in the Senate on whether to convict the president of the impeachment charges, thereby ordering him out of office.

Many observers believe that's not likely to happen, since a two-thirds vote in the Senate is required, and even though Republicans admit that he did in fact say and do the things listed in the impeachment charges.

Some observers also suggest that even if the Senate does vote to convict, the president may refuse to leave. That would cause a major crisis, both nationally and politically as well as constitutionally. The alternative may be that the Senate vote a formal censure of the president, an expression of their disapproval but short of ousting him from office.

Typically, the president's speech was interrupted repeatedly by applause, but observers stopped counting the number of interruptions several presidents ago after it became clear that the interruptions were not spontaneous but were led by members of the president's team.

This year, the president's speech was punctuated by applause after nearly every sentence. Moreover, the applause did not gradually subside, but stopped instantly, a clear sign that it was being led by a single conductor.

A Date to Live in History
5 February 2020

Not guilty.

To no one's surprise, the Senate voted to acquit the president of the charges filed against him in the articles of impeachment. What was a surprise, however, was that Mitt Romney, a Republican senator from Utah and a former presidential candidate, voted "guilty" on the first of the two impeachment charges -- abuse of power.

The repercussions of his decision may well be abusive against him and his family, but he cited his religious beliefs in the importance of right and wrong that were a major factor in his decision. Romney is a devout Mormon.

The final vote was 52-48, as more than half the senators voted for acquittal. Conviction would require a two-thirds majority -- 67 guilty votes.

On the second charge, defiance of subpoenas and obstruction of Congress, Romney voted with his fellow Republicans to clear the president of the allegation that defiance of congressional subpoenas equaled abuse of power. The final vote on that charge was 53 not guilty, and 47 guilty.

Many of the president's supporters acknowledge that he did in fact do many of the things he was accused of doing in the impeachment charges, but that they did not rise to the level needed to remove him from office.

Instead, they said, the decision should be left up to voters in the coming election. To convict him now and remove him from office, they argued, would be to nullify the previous election.

A swift reaction from editorialists hinged largely on the idea that the verdict amounted to permission for the president -- any president -- to do whatever he likes, regardless of law or tradition. Or, as Trump himself claimed, "Article Two of the Constitution says I can do whatever I want."

The White House said the president would make a public announcement on his reaction tomorrow, Thursday, February 6.

Sore Winner
6 February 2020

The president celebrated his victory over an impeachment attempt with an hour-long rambling diatribe against his critics, live on nationwide television, heavy on insults and sprinkled with an obscenity.

He entered the East Room of the White House to a recording of "Hail to the chief, who in triumph advances," preceded by four Ruffles and Flourishes, a musical salute usually reserved for formal occasions.

Whether this was an occasion important enough to justify the use of the musical salute usually reserved for the formal entrance of the chief of state, or that it was a bid by Team Trump to salve his bruised ego is another question.

Listeners were reminded of the chant of "Four more years" when he entered the House of Representatives for his State of the Union speech, as well as the chant of "Hail Trump" used by some of his white nationalist supporters during another rally in November 2016, soon after his election.

Earlier, he attacked his opponents during a speech

to the yearly Prayer Breakfast sponsored by religious organizations. This brought criticism from many observers that the remarks were inappropriate, and that he should have focused instead on the need to accept difficulties, learn from them and move on.

Also this morning, House Speaker Nancy Pelosi called his State of the Union speech "beneath the dignity of the White House and an insult" to the House of Representatives to use the venue for a campaign rally speech.

At the beginning of the session, the president refused to greet Pelosi with a handshake as he handed her a copy of his speech. And at the end of the speech, Pelosi tore up her copy.

When questioned about that, she called the speech "a manifest of mistruths." She listed some of them, especially his claim that he inherited an economy that was "a mess." Rather, she pointed out that the recovery from the Great Recession had begun during his predecessor's term, and that "he inherited a momentum," which is continuing.

And during his celebratory speech in the East Room of the White House, rather than offer some hope for a better relationship with Congress, he offered instead "an apology to my family for having to go through a phony and rotten deal by some very sick people."

The East Room was packed with supporters of the president, and media representatives were restricted to the back of the room.

Conclusion and Prediction
7 February 2020

Public and news media attention will now focus on the election campaign and how the president will translate his victory over impeachment to approval of his strategy and tactics in treating those who disagree with him.

Some observers compare the president's attitudes and comments to those of a dictator attempting to solidify his control of government, while others see the decline and fall of the Republican Party.

Meanwhile, there is the possibility that Sen. Mitt Romney (R-Utah), a devout Mormon who split with party unity to vote "Guilty" in the impeachment trial, will appeal to other Republicans who acknowledge the president's wrong-doing but insist it fell short of removing him from office. These nay-sayers suggest it will be up to voters in the November presidential election to do that.

With that in mind, there is the possibility that the party will reject Trump and nominate Romney as its candidate for president. Or that the party will split, with one of the aspirants forming a new political party. That split could well assure a Democratic victory in November. And in a longer view, the Republican Party itself may expire as a viable political party.

Stay tuned.

www.ingramcontent.com/pod-product-compliance
Lightning Source LLC
Chambersburg PA
CBHW051124250726
48655CB00007B/2864